CRAP DIVINATION

Dingleberry Marx

An Hachette UK Company
www.hachette.co.uk

First published in Great Britain in 2021 by Pyramid,
an imprint of Octopus Publishing Group Ltd
Carmelite House, 50 Victoria Embankment, London EC4Y 0DZ
www.octopusbooks.co.uk

Distributed in the US by
Hachette Book Group
1290 Avenue of the Americas
4th and 5th Floors
New York, NY 10104

Distributed in Canada by
Canadian Manda Group
664 Annette St.
Toronto, Ontario, Canada M6S 2C8

ISBN 978-0-7537-3467-4

A CIP catalogue record for this book is available from the British Library

Printed and bound in China

10 9 8 7 6 5 4 3 2 1

Publisher: Lucy Pessell
Designer: Hannah Coughlin
Editor: Sarah Kennedy
Editorial Assistant: Emily Martin
Senior Production Manager: Peter Hunt

Illustrations: 123rf.com/Anton Burakov; hydognik; Iulia Brovchenko; maximus25;
Michelle Still; Pavel Stasevich; shutterstock.com/ArtemSh

CRAP DIVINATION

DIVINATION

THE DARK ART OF READING DARK MARKS:

how to interpret toilet runes

Dingleberry Marx

If there is light,
there must be dark.

Let me help you sift
through the crap and find
the sweetcorn of truth.

For millennia people have searched the world, the skies, and even searched their teacups in the hope of glimpsing their future, when all along we should have been looking to what comes from within, that which comes from our souls.

Let's reaffirm that now with a simple chant to remind us what is truly at the heart of life's mysteries. Say it out loud:

Our Souls, Our Souls, Our Souls.

I present the turd teller's tarot, the butt-bean favomancer's friend, the smelly-pebble pessomancer's pamphlet: this is The Dark Art of Reading Dark Marks.

BINGLEBERRY MARX

GREAT LUCIFER'S MERKIN

The first recorded sighting of this harbinger was by Andrew Rodshed, an amateur chartered accountant from Leicestershire, UK.

Upon turning and regarding the sight in his porcelain oracle he exclaimed, "Great Lucifer's merkin!" giving this sign its moniker.

As you will no doubt have noticed, there is an unusual haze around this sign. There is a waft of ambiguity. It could go either way.

Find a cat and place a mint leaf on its head before next Tuesday and the spirits will be allayed.

CACA MOUSSAKA

There are many layers to this mark.

There's a big difference
between knowing your shit and
knowing you're shit.

On this occasion, it turns out
you are shit. Ask anyone.

SAUCY SEESAW
SAUCISSON

Depending on your dominant
butt-cheek, this arc of prophecy could
lead one of two ways.

When you sit astride the
seesaw of shite you may be lifted up
but someone else must fall.

Choose your nemesis and
await further signs.

Also, remember to peel
bananas before you eat them.

THE DARK WIZARD

The moon is cusping Uranus as it moves into a monthly gooch.

This will lead directly to you being "cancelled" over a simple misunderstanding involving dressing up as a ghost.

In tasseomancy, a pointy hat is an indication that psychic work will be successful. In this book, it's confirmation that I know my shit.

WHAT THE DEUCE?

Oh wow! I mean ... oof! You did that?!
What's wrong with you?! Have some
self-respect! Jeez.

Like your friend's kid's art,
no-one wants to see this.

However, if it does present itself
you must take on more "spirit
sustenance", which happens to be
found in all high-fibre foods.

MUDDY WATERS

You have been visited by
food's evil cousin.

I see a trip to the doctor
in your future.

To take care of number one, first you
have to take care of number two.

METEOWRONG

Do you have internal demons?
Or is it just your duodenum?

If you see this mark you
probably just fell off the toilet.

Get up, mate, you're
embarrassing yourself.

EL BURRITO

Some say it is just a legend spread by
gauchos and cowboys as they warm
their beans on the fire. Some dare
speak its name ... El Burrito!

It has been told that if you see
the face of El Burrito in your bowl then
you have 24 hours before El Burrito
returns ... into you.

So, good luck with that.

If the image appears upside down,
you've just dropped a dead donkey.

THE BEAST WITH THE BROWN EYE

This mark augurs disaster
for the whole village.

Quickly, gather the elders! Light the
beacon! Tell the aldermen!

Whatever you do, do NOT
look in the mirror!

GATHERING CLOUDS

This is an absolute classic.
As you can see, there are three foxes.
Two of them have just exploded and
the other one is raging.

This isn't one of those metaphorical
ones or anything like that – just be
extremely wary of foxes for the next
seven days.

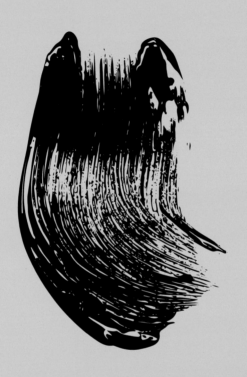

THE REARING
SHADOOBY SLUG

Your dabblings with the five-minute
miracle diet have proved successful.

Congratulations, you just
lost weight.

DOCTOR POOSE

With a poo on the loo
And this glob of doo-doo
The fate you await
Is more hullabaloo!
Is this mark an old shark?
Or a tracing of bark?
Is this blob here to warn?
Or a piece of sweetcorn?
Are the lines at the side
My unbearable pride?
Is that bit next to "Shanks"
My existential angst?
To find the answer
Follow your noses!
Now ask yourself:
Does it smell like roses?

THE HOSTAGE

To see vertical lines like these
indicates that you feel trapped
and imprisoned.

You need to make positive
changes in your life.

The reverse meaning is that you
have recently released something you
have held captive for some time.
Well done you.

If the lines are going in the
other direction then you're
doing it wrong.

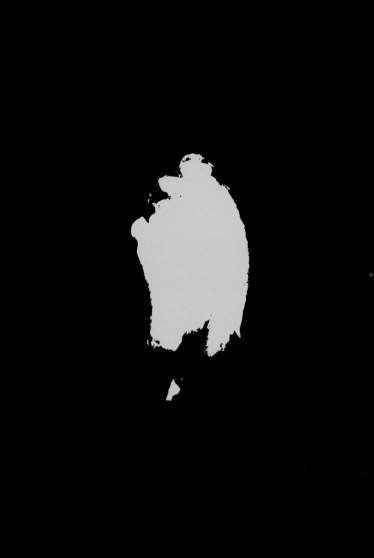

POOP DU JOUR

Same old shit.

Tomorrow will bring same shit,
different day.

Just because it comes from inside you,
doesn't mean it's not shit!

THIS SHIT IS BIBLICAL

After less examination, I have found
out that a lot of the Bible is just about
not getting the shits.
Is this the reason for its success?

If you've ever had food poisoning,
this book will have suddenly become
very precious to you. When you've got
it coming out both ends - spewing and
shitting seeming universes of awfulness -
you'd believe that anything stopping this
must be a miracle.

THE CAULDRON

The witches are stirring the
blind-eel stew. Don't stray far
from the bowl for an hour or so.

This is real mud goblin
turd-word magickery:

You can't spell "secretion" without
the word "secret". And, "his secrets"
is an anagram of "shit recess".

Fact: The cat was worshipped in
ancient Egypt; the French for cat is
"chat". Shat. Think about that.

Coincidence? I say no.

THE TOWER OF STERCORE!

An ill omen, The Tower of Stercore predicts that you are going to have to take so much shit today.

Acres of shit. Fathoms.
It'll be like wading through a marathon of arse gravy before then having to go back because you forgot your keys.

I'd consider going back to bed.

DE BEAUVOIR'S GUSSET

In divination, the arch represents
a passage and new openings.

It may also suggest a
new direction.

I can confirm this:
you have sat backwards on the
porcelain throne.

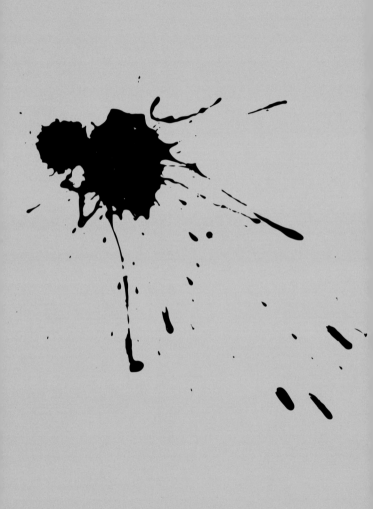

POLLOCKS

Pollocks show you have a need
for self-expression.

Maybe you should consider
taking up a creative hobby: knitting;
painting; throwing stones at a picture
of your ex on an old abandoned
industrial estate. Whatever gets your
creative juices flowing!

If there are several of these
it is a load of Pollocks.

And your Nan's on the phone.

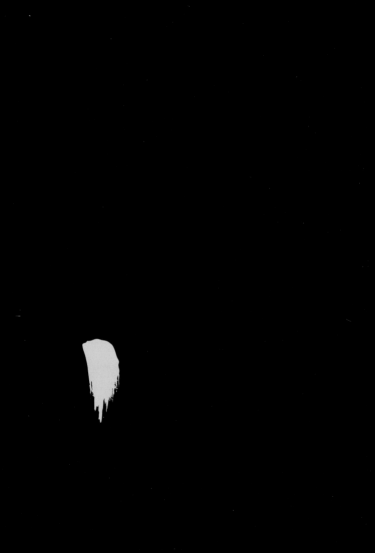

POP GOES THE WEASEL!

There was no messing about here,
was there? Good job.

Don't be smug; you're about
to lose a toenail.

THE SHITTING FORECAST

The splooge is rising in your
chart – easterly, north-easterly – and
it's twinning with some
blooble-blubbles in North Utsire,
Cromarty, South Utsire ... prevailing
Gails and dogging.

Try to catch a glimpse if you can.

CHLOROTHON THE UNBELIEVER

This means that you are the
type of person who would only get an
electric car because "then they can't
hear me coming".

There is an aura around you.
A smelly aura.

ROYAL FLUSH

Someone is going to
shout at the Queen.

This shouldn't affect you too
much unless you're the Queen.

If you aren't the Queen but
believe you are, you have some
serious shit to work through.

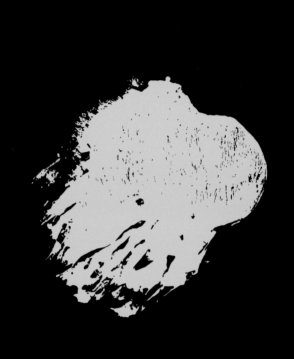

OUR SOUL FOOD

Did you cook up this little pudding?
Well this means it's time you gave
yourself a bit more attention.

And here's the recipe!

Just take two parts patronising tripe
and mix with one part unmerited
praise. Then take a large dollop of
preying on your fears and really rub
it in. Next, just whisk in a load of
unrealistic expectations and top it off
with a bukkake of "You're unique".

Mmm ... delicious!

THE BLEEDING HEART

The maker of this mark will see
The Bleeding Heart; slashed with barbs
and spewing blood.

This means that you're going to feel
really sorry for yourself.

Oh, you want more, don't you?
Always more!

"Oooh can I get that in mystical,
please?", "Have you got those
socks in an illusion of spirituality,
pleeeeeease?"

No! They come in grey!

Confucius says your shit stinks.

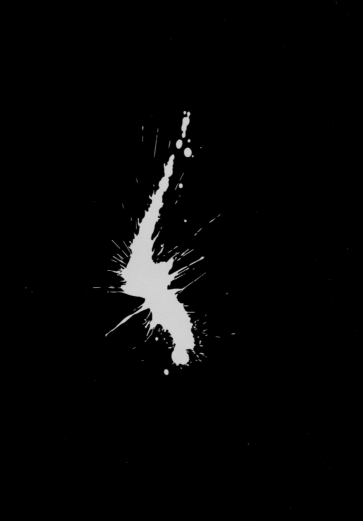

NUMBER TWO'S COMPANY

Numerology is an ancient belief
in divine or mystical relationships
between numbers and life events.

In this case, it's the number two.
However, it is not the only
number involved here.

Look at your sample again.
Squint your eyes a bit. That's it.
Just relax your focus slightly.

Now, imagine you can see the
number four. You can see the number
four, can't you? That's right. In the
coming days you should give undue
significance to the number four.

Pay heed, pay heed, for you
did the deed!

BENEDICT
BUMBERSPLASH

You're great, you know that?
Don't listen to them,
you're awesome!

This proves it, doesn't it?
This mark? Y'know?
You're just ... you're just great;
they don't know what they're
talking about.

YOU CAN CALL
ME POLYVAGAL

In this work we can clearly see the
shape of a triangle; great in snooker
and chocolate but often troublesome
in relationships.

There are three in this relationship
when there should be two:
Number 1: You
Number 2: Your number two

Time to cut corners and wipe
away the excess.

FREUD'S SPLATULA

An ambiguous one, this.
Perhaps you're repressing something.

This represents a Freudian flip,
as well as a penis. It signals a
sea-change in your life.

You will stop fancying your
mom and start fancying your dad
instead, or vice versa depending on
where the moon is in your cycle.

Interesting fact:
Freud's mom was actually well fit.

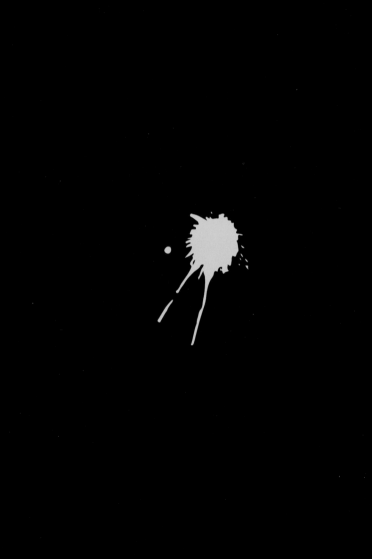

BUMFIRE NIGHT

With this display you do indeed have
fireworks on the way!

This poo-pipe pyrotechnic
pertains to potential pillow pals
popping off pant parties!

With new lovers, as with fireworks,
wear protection and if it doesn't work
out the first time, never go back.

THE ACE OF SPADES

Oh baby, you hit the jackpot here!

This is just incredible;
you're so lucky!

The joy that awaits you will be
unparalleled! This is basically the best
one. This is unbelievable!

In fact, actually, I don't
believe you. You didn't get that!
You?! Come on! No way you got this;
you're not good enough.

Go back three spaces.

URANUS IN TRANSIT

I know what you're thinking:
"Look at that! As if I wasn't in enough
trouble what with Mercury being
in retrograde!"

Now, as we can all see as clear as
day, so is Uranus and, as we all know,
Uranus's movement is generational, so
settle in because this crap is going to
go on for ages.

Don't flip your lid; just sit back,
relax and let Uranus do the work.

THE FLOOSH OF GAIA

Ah, yes, this augurs ... heavily.
Strong, strong, augurs.

Those augurs at the top are
super augury. There's so much
auguring going on here.
You've got some of the best augurs
I've seen in a long time.
Check out the augurs on that!

I wouldn't even worry about it.

JUNG MAN (THERE'S NO NEED TO FEEL DOWN)

As a schoolboy, Carl Jung had a vision. It was a vision of God, seated on a golden throne, unleashing "an enormous turd" on a cathedral.

Is this what helped him realise that we not only shape our history, and what we leave behind us, but are also shaped by it?

We will never know for sure, because he did tend to tell the odd porkie-pie, but I think it just might have been.

Sometimes it's not your shit that's the problem, it's the collective shit. So don't be so hard on yourself; blame your family.

LUTHER'S REVENGE

Martin Luther, 1483-1546, was a German theologian and avid toilet user.

It seems quite the convenience that Luther came across so much new information whilst spending hours alone in his privy. While Martin claimed to have terrible constipation, some think that Luther actually gained his wisdom the old way: bending before the bowl.

It is said that Luther did indeed glimpse the future and saw that he wasn't even going to be the best Martin Luther. This may be what led to Luther challenging the Pope, saying that the Bible is the only source of divinely revealed knowledge, inferring that you should not dabble in the dark, thus keeping the secret of his wisdom safe.

Luther was right to be wary. As Leviticus himself said; "You shall not interpret omens or tell fortunes. You shall not round off the hair on your temples or mar the edge of your beard."

See, divination is almost as bad as being a hipster or having bangs.

This brings us to our message: maybe you should get a haircut.

THE GHOST OF OLD STINKY'S CHUTNEY MINE

They know your secret. Get out.
Get out now!

THE HAND OF GOD

Often misinterpreted, this simply
means you did a trump whilst abluting,
as shown by the small hand print.

What are you doing? Don't do that.

Maybe you should go outside
from now on.

NOW FLUSH AND WASH
YER HANDS YA DIRTY GIT.
AND REMEMBER: DON'T
BELIEVE ANY OLD SHIT.